◄ This art museum in Spain is made of metal.

Contents

Build Background   **4**
Sensing the World

1 Understand the Big Idea   **6**
Is It Matter?

2 Take a Closer Look   **16**
Iron at Work

3 Make Connections   **24**

Extend Learning   **30**

Glossary   **34**

Index   **36**

BOOK DESIGN/PHOTO RESEARCH
3R1 Group, Inc.

Published by the National Geographic Society
Washington, D.C. 20036-4688

Product No. 4T60318

ISBN-13: 978-0-7922-5442-3
ISBN-10: 0-7922-5442-2

Printed in Canada

2012
10 9 8 7 6 5 4 3 2

Sensing the World

The Five Senses

Touch

Taste

What Is Matter?

Glen Phelan

Produced through the worldwide resources of the National Geographic Society, John M. Fahey, Jr., President and Chief Executive Officer; Gilbert M. Grosvenor, Chairman of the Board; Nina D. Hoffman, Executive Vice President and President, Books and Education Publishing Group.

PREPARED BY NATIONAL GEOGRAPHIC SCHOOL PUBLISHING

Ericka Markman, Senior Vice President and President, Children's Books and Education Publishing Group; Steve Mico, Senior Vice President, Editorial Director, Publisher; Francis Downey, Executive Editor; Richard Easby, Editorial Manager; Bea Jackson, Director of Layout and Design; Jim Hiscott, Design Manager; Cynthia Olson, Art Director; Margaret Sidlosky, Illustrations Director; Matt Wascavage, Manager of Publishing Services; Sean Philpotts, Jane Ponton, Production Managers; Ted Tucker, Production Specialist.

MANUFACTURING AND QUALITY CONTROL

Christopher A. Liedel, Chief Financial Officer; Phillip L. Schlosser, Director; Clifton M. Brown III, Manager

CONSULTANT AND REVIEWER

Jordan D. Marché II, Ph.D., University of Wisconsin-Madison

BOOK DEVELOPMENT

Amy Sarver

How do you find out about things? You use your five senses. Your senses are touch, taste, hearing, sight, and smell.

Your senses give you information. For example, you can see, touch, smell, and taste an apple. You can even tap an apple with your finger. That lets you hear what it sounds like. Your senses help you explore everything around you.

Look at the pictures.

- What senses are being used in each photo?

- How do your senses help you learn about objects around you?

Hearing

Sight

Smell

Big Idea
The world is made of matter.

Set Purpose
Learn what matter is and how it can be described.

Is It

Questions You Will Explore

How can you describe matter?
How can you measure matter?

Matter?

Look left, right, up, and down. You are surrounded by many things. Did you know that all the things around you are made of **matter**? This book is matter. The air you breathe is matter. Everything that has **mass** and takes up space is matter.

In this book, you will learn what matter is and how to describe matter.

matter – anything that has mass and takes up space

mass – the amount of matter in something

What Is Matter?

Can you picture yourself in a hot-air balloon?
What a view! You are high in the air. The land
is far below you. You see clouds floating by.
All of these things have something in common.
The balloon, air, clouds, and you are all made
of matter.

▼ Hot-air balloons,
clouds, and air
are all matter.

hot-air balloon ▶

What Is Not Matter?

Is there anything that is not matter? Yes!
Sound is not matter. An instrument, such as a
violin, is matter. But the sound it makes is not.

What else is not matter? Heat! The logs on a
fire are matter. But the heat from the fire is not.

▲ Sound is not matter.

▲ The heat from this fire is not matter.

Properties of Matter

All matter can be described. How could you describe the cherries in the picture? You could use **properties** to tell about them. For example, you could describe their size and shape. These are properties of the cherries.

property – something about an object that can be observed or measured

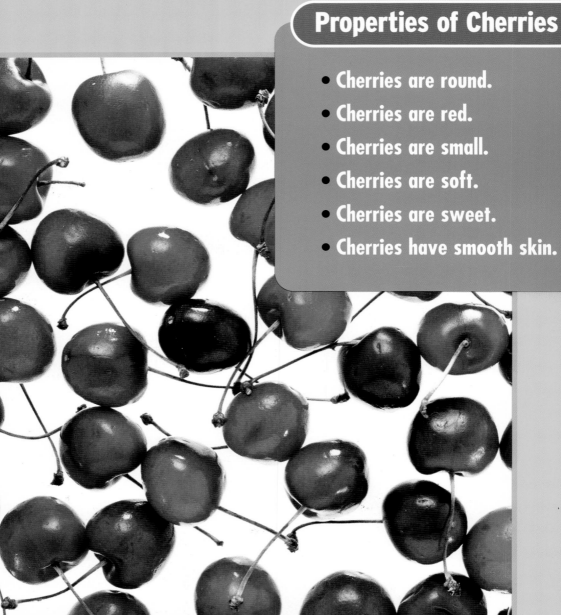

Properties of Cherries

- Cherries are round.
- Cherries are red.
- Cherries are small.
- Cherries are soft.
- Cherries are sweet.
- Cherries have smooth skin.

States of Matter

State is another property of matter. A state is a form of matter. Solid, liquid, and gas are three states of matter. Solids have a set shape and **volume.** Volume is the amount of space something takes up. Ice is a solid. Liquids have a set volume but not a set shape. Water is a liquid. Gases do not have a set shape or volume. Steam is a gas. State is a property that tells about an object's shape and volume.

state – a form of matter, such as solid, liquid, or gas

volume – the amount of space something takes up

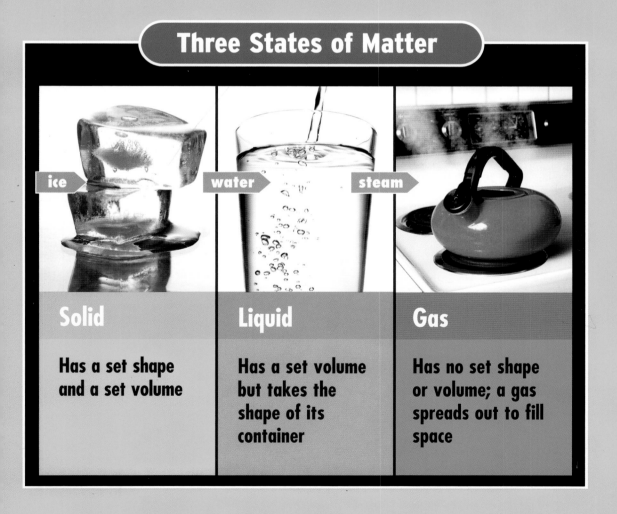

Three States of Matter

Solid
Has a set shape and a set volume

Liquid
Has a set volume but takes the shape of its container

Gas
Has no set shape or volume; a gas spreads out to fill space

Measuring Properties

Some properties of matter can be measured. Mass is a property of matter. Mass is the amount of matter in something. Mass can be measured. Mass is measured in units called **grams.**

....

gram – a unit of mass

▼ **This scale measures the mass of the candy.**

12

What Is Volume?

Volume is another property that can be measured. Volume is the amount of space something takes up. A beaker is a tool that measures a liquid's volume. Volume can be measured in units called **liters**.

....

liter – a unit of volume

▲ **A beaker is a tool that measures volume.**

beaker

▲ **A beaker measures the volume of this liquid.**

What Is Density?

An object with a large volume does not always have a large mass. For example, a beach ball takes up more space than a bowling ball. But the beach ball is filled with air. The bowling ball is solid matter. The bowling ball has more mass in its volume. So the bowling ball has a greater **density**. To find an object's density, just divide its mass by its volume. An object's density is measured in grams per liter.

....

density – the mass per unit volume of an object or substance

Comparing Mass, Volume, and Density

Ball	Mass	Volume	Density
beach ball	100 grams	113 liters	100 grams ÷ 113 liters = .8 grams/liter
bowling ball	4,500 grams	5 liters	4,500 grams ÷ 5 liters = 900 grams/liter

Properties Are Useful

Properties, such as density, help you figure out uses for things. For example, the beach ball's density lets it float on water. So the beach ball is perfect for games in water.

Think about metals. Metals have some important properties. Most metals can be formed into different shapes. Metals are strong. They are also good **conductors**. That means they are good at carrying heat or electricity. These properties make metals useful.

....

conductor – a material through which heat or electricity flows easily

Stop and Think!

What are some ways you can describe matter?

▲ A metal radiator is a good conductor of heat.

▼ These metal gears are strong and have different shapes.

Recap
Explain how properties
of matter can be useful.

Set Purpose
Learn about the
properties of metal.

Iron
at W

▼ A blacksmith shapes a piece of iron with a hammer.

ork

Many metals are useful. Each kind of metal is good for certain jobs. Let's take a look at the properties of one kind of metal—iron.

Iron Long Ago

In 1922, a scientist discovered the tomb of King Tutankhamun. He was an ancient Egyptian king. He lived more than 3,200 years ago. His tomb was filled with objects made of silver, gold, and jewels.

One of the most interesting objects in the tomb was a knife. The knife had a blade made of iron. To the ancient Egyptians, iron was more valuable than gold. It was the strongest metal they had. It was perfect for tools and weapons.

Today, iron is very common. But in ancient Egypt, it was very rare. The Egyptians had not learned how to find large amounts of iron. They did not have many things made from iron.

▶ The blade of King Tutankhamun's knife was made of iron.

▶ This gold mask shows the face of King Tutankhamun.

Iron From Space

The first iron that people used might have come from meteorites. These are chunks of rock and metal that travel through space and crash into Earth.

Ancient people might have broken off iron from meteorites. Then people heated and hammered the metal into different shapes. One of those shapes might have been the blade of Tutankhamun's knife.

▼ **This large meteorite is made of iron and nickel.**

Iron Ore

Over time, people discovered iron in rocks.
Rock that contains iron is called iron ore.
People learned to heat iron ore. The heat
changed the iron from a solid to a liquid.
Then the liquid iron poured out of the rock.

When the iron cooled, it became a solid again.
It could be hammered into tools. But the iron
was not very strong.

▼ **This ancient ax is made of iron.**

▼ **Rock that contains iron is called iron ore.**

iron ore

An Important Discovery

Later, a group of people called the Hittites made an amazing discovery. They heated and cooled the iron ore many times. The iron got harder and stronger.

The iron was mixing with carbon. The carbon came from the wood used to heat the iron ore. The added carbon turned the iron into steel. Steel is a much stronger metal than iron.

▼ Steel is made of iron mixed with carbon and other materials.

steel

Metal Mixtures

People have found many uses for steel. Steel is an **alloy**. An alloy is created by mixing a metal with another material. The material could be a metal, such as nickel. Or it could be a nonmetal, such as carbon.

An alloy has properties different from the materials that make it up. For example, iron is a somewhat weak metal. Carbon is lightweight and breakable. But mix them together, and you have strong, hard steel!

alloy – a mixture of two or more metals or a metal and a nonmetal

▼ **This hot, liquid steel is an alloy.**

Steel at Work

▼ Steel building

Steel is always made of iron and carbon. But steel can have different amounts of iron, carbon, and other materials. Each combination makes a different kind of steel. Each kind of steel has properties that make it good for certain uses.

Some steel is used for making huge buildings and bridges. Other kinds of steel are used to make cars and airplanes. Steel is also used to make paper clips. Steel is matter that people really put to use!

▶ Steel used in cars

Stop and Think!

What properties of steel make it useful?

▶ Steel paper clips

23

Recap

Explain how the properties of iron and steel are useful.

Set Purpose

Read these articles to learn more about metals and matter.

CONNECT WHAT YOU HAVE LEARNED

Matter

Matter is all around you. Even you are made of matter. Matter is anything that has mass and volume.

Here are some ideas you learned about matter.

- Matter has properties that you can observe and describe.
- Properties of matter can be measured.
- Solid, liquid, and gas are three states of matter.
- Properties can help people find uses for different kinds of matter.

Check What You Have Learned

What does each picture show about matter?

▲ Cherries have properties that you can describe.

▲ The mass of these candies is measured on a scale.

▲ The water in the pitcher is a liquid.

▲ This bridge is made of strong steel.

Precious **Metals**

People have treasured gold and silver for many years. These metals are precious because of their properties.

Gold and silver have a beautiful color and shine. Gold almost looks like it glows. And it stays shiny. Some gold objects were made thousands of years ago. The gold is as shiny now as it was when the objects were made.

Gold and silver are quite rare, too. That means there is not a lot of gold and silver on Earth. So gold and silver are very valuable.

▲ **Silver teapot**

◀ **Gold bars**

A Bronze Bell

The Liberty Bell in Philadelphia is made of an alloy called bronze. It is made of copper, tin, and other materials. Bronze has properties different from the metals that make it up. For example, copper and tin are soft, weak metals. But when they are mixed together with other materials, they make strong bronze!

▲ The Liberty Bell in Philadelphia is made of an alloy called bronze.

An Attractive Metal

magnetite

▶ **Magnetite attracts metals.**

CONNECT TO THE FUTURE

High-Tech Metals

▶**The hot rocket engines on this spacecraft are made of titanium.**

Scientists are always developing new uses for metals and alloys. One metal that has become more and more useful is titanium. It is very strong, yet very lightweight. It does not rust easily. It can also keep its shape when it is very hot. These properties make titanium very useful. For example, titanium is used to make rocket engines.

In Greece, there is a myth about a shepherd boy named Magnes. One day, Magnes was walking on some rocks. Suddenly, he stopped. He could not move. He looked down. The iron nails in his sandals were stuck to the rock below his feet!

Magnes found a kind of rock we now call magnetite. It has the property of attracting anything with a lot of iron in it. So magnetite is a magnet. Both the words *magnetite* and *magnet* were named after Magnes.

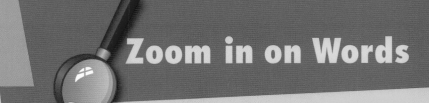

Many kinds of words are used in this book.
Here you will learn about homophones. You will
also learn about multiple-meaning words.

Homophones

Homophones are words that sound alike but have different
meanings. Find the homophones below. Then write a new
sentence for each homophone.

This **steel** is rolled into thin
sheets.

Thieves **steal** things that do not
belong to them.

Iron **ore** is rock that contains iron.

He can hold the sand **or** let it fall
from his hands.

Multiple-Meaning Words

Multiple-meaning words are words that have more than one meaning. Find the multiple-meaning words below. Then write a new sentence for each multiple-meaning word.

The pan is made of **iron.**

The **iron** takes the wrinkles out of the shirt.

They **hammer** the metal into a flat sheet.

She hit the nail with the **hammer.**

The hot-air balloon takes up a lot of **space.**

There are many stars in **space.**

Write About Matter

Research a solid, a liquid, or a gas. Find out about an example of one state of matter. Then write a poem that describes the example you chose.

Research
Collect books and reference materials, or go online.

Read and Take Notes
As you read, take notes and draw pictures.

Write
Then write a poem about your example. Begin by listing words that describe the example. Include any words that come to mind when you think of that kind of matter. Then use some or all of the words in a poem.

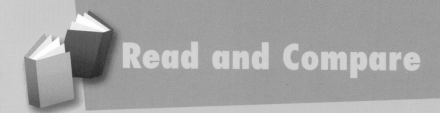
Read More About Matter

Find and read other books about matter. As you read, think about these questions.

- What is matter?
- How do different states of matter compare?
- How do scientists study matter?

Books to Read

▲ Read about matter and its properties.

▲ Read about how matter can change.

▲ Read about forces that move matter.

Glossary

alloy (page 22)
A mixture of two or more metals or a metal and a nonmetal
Steel is an alloy of iron, carbon, and other materials.

conductor (page 15)
A material through which heat or electricity flows easily
Metal is a good conductor.

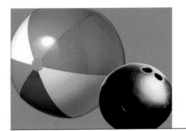

density (page 14)
The mass per unit volume of an object or substance
The bowling ball has a greater density than the beach ball.

gram (page 12)
A unit of mass
The candy had a mass of ten grams.

liter (page 13)
A unit of volume
The pitcher holds one liter of liquid.

mass (page 7)
The amount of matter in something
Mass is measured with this scale.

matter (page 7)
Anything that has mass and takes up space
This building is made of matter.

property (page 10)
Something about an object that can be observed
or measured
Cherries have properties that can be observed.

state (page 11)
A form of matter, such as solid, liquid, or gas
Ice is water in a solid state.

volume (page 11)
The amount of space something takes up
The lemonade in the pitcher has volume.

Index

alloy	22, 27–28, 34
conductor	15, 34
density	14–15, 34
gas	11, 24, 32
iron ore	20–21
liquid	11, 13, 20, 24–25, 32
mass	7, 12, 14, 24–25, 35
matter	6–12, 14–16, 32–33, 35
metal	15–24, 26–29
meteorite	19
property	10–13, 15–17, 22–29, 33, 35
solid	11, 14, 20, 24, 32
state	11, 24, 32, 35
steel	21–23, 25, 30
volume	11, 13–14, 24, 35